a million
voices for
nature

Cardiff Libraries
www.cardiff.gov.uk/librari·

Llyfrgelloedd Caerdydd
www.caerdydd.gov.uk/llyfrgelloedd

D1148263

Mike Dilger

WILD TOWN

Wildlife on your doorstep

A & C BLACK • LONDON

ACC. No: 03097767

Published 2012 by
A&C Black
An imprint of Bloomsbury Publishing Plc
50 Bedford Square, London, WC1B 3DP

www.bloomsbury.com

ISBN 978-1-4081-7390-9

Copyright © 2012 Bloomsbury Publishing Plc
Text copyright © 2012 Mike Dilger

The right of Mike Dilger to be identified as the author of this work has been asserted by him in accordance with
the Copyrights, Designs and Patents Act 1988.

A CIP catalogue for this book is available from the British Library.

All photographs © Shutterstock, except: p4-5 Laurent Geslin/naturepl.com; p6-7 © David Tipling/naturepl.com;
p10-11 © Terry Whittaker/2020VISION/naturepl.com; p18 © Laurent Geslin/naturepl.com; p18-19 © Delpho/
ARCO/naturepl.com; p19 © Alan Williams/naturepl.com; p26-27 © Laurent Geslin/naturepl.com; p36-37 ©
David Tipling/naturepl.com; p41 (top) © Strobilomyces via Wikimedia Commons; p41 (bottom) Eike Wulfmeyer
via Wikimedia Commons; p44-45 © Terry Whittaker/2020VISION/naturepl.com; p49 © Sarah via Wikimedia
Commons; p50 © Dietmar Nill/naturepl.com; p51 (top) © Dietmar Nill/naturepl.com; p58-59 © Laurent Geslin/
naturepl.com; p66 © L. B. Tettenborn via Wikimedia Commons; p69 (middle) © Viridiflavus via Wikimedia
Commons; p70-71 © Terry Whittaker/2020VISION/naturepl.com; p84-85 © Andy Rouse/naturepl.com; p90-91 ©
Michael Hutchinson/naturepl.com; p98-99 © Andy Sands/naturepl.com; p100-101 © Michael Hutchinson/naturepl.
com; p106 © Frank Vincentz via Wikimedia Commons; p107 (top) © Enrico Blasutto via Wikimedia Commons;
p107 (bottom) © Walter Siegmund via Wikimedia Commons; p110-111 © Michel Poinsignon/naturepl.com; p112-
113 © Dave Bevan/naturepl.com; p113 Adrian Davies/naturepl.com; p114-115 © Stephen Dalton/naturepl.com;
p115 © Steve Packham/naturepl.com; p118 Alan Williams/naturepl.com; p122-123 © Ernie Janes/naturepl.com;
p127 courtesy of Piotr Naskrecki via Wikimedia Commons; © p128 (bottom) Adrian Davies/naturepl.com; p129
(bottom) Philippe Clement/naturepl.com; p130-131 © Laurent Geslin/naturepl.com; p140-141 © Paul Hobson/
naturepl.com; p155 (top) © Joseph Berger via Wikimedia Commons; p155 (bottom) Kim Taylor/naturepl.com;
p156-157 © Stephen Dalton/naturepl.com.

Cover: front centre © Laurent Geslin/naturepl.com; far left © Laurent Geslin/naturepl.com; left © Laurent Geslin/
naturepl.com; right © Stephen Dalton/naturepl.com; far right © Laurent Geslin/naturepl.com; back © Michael
Hutchinson/naturepl.com; inside back flap © Mike Dilger.

Copyright in the photographs remains with the individuals and organisations credited above. Every effort has
been made to trace copyright holders and obtain their permission for use of copyright material. The publishers
would be pleased to rectify any error or omission in future editions.

All rights reserved. No part of this publication may be reproduced in any form or by any means – graphic,
electronic or mechanical, including photocopying, recording, taping or information storage and retrieval systems –
without the prior permission in writing of the publishers.

This book is produced using paper that is made from wood grown in managed, sustainable forests.

It is natural, renewable and recyclable. The logging and manufacturing processes
conform to the environmental regulations of the country of origin.

Printed in China by C&C Offset Printing Co., Ltd.

10 9 8 7 6 5 4 3 2 1

MIX
Paper from
responsible sources
FSC® C008047
FSC
www.fsc.org

CONTENTS

INTRODuCTION

You may think your town is a wildlife-free zone, but you'd be wrong.

Many animals have decided that towns and cities aren't that different from their original homes. To a peregrine falcon, a tower block can look very similar to a tall cliff, and lots of foxes have decided the 'urban jungle' is just as good a place to live as wooded countryside.

In this book, find out what might live or grow near you on buildings, bridges, railway lines and in parks, get top tips about where to spot your local wildlife and learn how your new neighbours find food and shelter on the town streets. Also, discover fascinating animal facts such as how the little owl protects its nest or which spider hitched a lift around the world in ships and trains to live in your house.

So why not take a look around your town or city? Our towns have a wild side and it's up to you to track it down!

THE URBAN DESERT: TOWN CENTRES

At first glance the town centre might seem like a dry urban desert of glass, metal and concrete with little or no space for wildlife. But look closer and there are all sorts of tough animals and plants which love our city streets.

FOX

The Fabulous Mr Fox is known by everyone, with his reddish-brown coat, bushy tail and big black-tipped ears. Foxes can be found in mountains, moorland, woodland and farmland. In the last 50 years foxes have discovered that town centres are full of ripe pickings to eat too.

SUPER SCAVENGERS

The key to their amazing urban success is an ability to eat virtually anything. Over half the diet of these super scavengers is made up of thrown-away food, which we leave in waste bins, dustbins or littered all over the floor. A hungry fox will polish off a half-eaten pizza, a curry or even a kebab without a second thought! Towns also offer plenty of places to hide out of sight during the day, whether resting under a garden shed or sunbathing on a roof.

FOX TALK

During the winter, as the mating season approaches, listen out for their barks and screams when you are tucked up in bed. Foxes use these sounds to keep in touch with each other. A female fox will usually give birth to a litter of four or five cubs in March, but they won't come out until May — after which it's playtime!

LIVING DANGEROUSLY

Urban foxes may take the occasional pet rabbit or chicken, but foxes and pet cats tend to keep away from each other. Sadly urban foxes often live fast and die young. Many don't even reach their second birthday before either being hit by a car or catching an unpleasant foxy disease called mange.

Fox lunchbox
An urban fox finds a tasty snack in a litterbin.

BROWN RAT

The brown rat sometimes seems to be one of the world's most hated animals, but it's also one of the toughest and most successful. Just 300 years ago, there were no brown rats in Britain at all. But when they finally made it across the English Channel, as stowaways on ships in the early eighteenth century, they swept into every town from Lands End to John O'Groats – and whether we like it or not, they are here to stay!

PERFECT HOMES

Our towns provide lots of food and shelter – they couldn't be any better suited for rats if they tried. Food stores and waste are easy pickings for this adaptable animal, whilst our sewers, other man-made tunnels and outbuildings provide the perfect places for them to hide out of sight until our backs are turned. Brown rats are also excellent at burrowing. They are super swimmers too – the brown rat would be a very successful competitor in the Animal Olympics!

A FAMILY AFFAIR

One of the most incredible things about the brown rat is how quickly it can breed. A female can produce five litters a year – around 50 babies in total – which will then be able to start breeding themselves at about three months old. Despite many rats being killed by cats, owls and foxes, it doesn't take a maths genius to work out why the British rat population is so huge. Whenever you are at ground level, you are never more than 50 metres from a rat.

FERAL PIGEON

Many years ago, you would have found the rock dove ancestors of these birds mostly on sea-cliffs and mountains. However, the feral pigeon has now swapped the cliffs and ledges of its original homes for the artificial ones in town centres.

CITY SLICKERS

Feral pigeons are experts in the art of scavenging stale bread from food outlets, taking bird-seed from tourists and begging the crust from your lunchtime sandwich. They have even developed super road sense and can dodge fearlessly between moving cars to pick up just a few crumbs.

PIGEON DATING

In towns, where the food supply is constant, pigeons will often breed all through the year. Look out for their amazing courtship rituals on a railway platform or street pavement. When it comes to romance, the males make all the moves. They puff out their neck feathers before approaching the female at a quick walking pace, whilst bowing, turning and cooing in an irresistible manner. Pigeon couples often mate for life.

TOP BIRD

Although they make a mess of our town centres with their droppings, and are sometimes dismissed as nothing more than 'flying rats', these fascinating birds deserve respect, as they are the closest many of us will ever come to a wild bird.

PEREGRINE FALCON

With its striking wings, handsome looks and incredible flying skills, the peregrine is without doubt one of Britain's true urban wildlife stars. Not only is it Britain's largest falcon, but with a diving speed of over 150 mph, this bird is also the fastest animal on the planet. There are 1,500 pairs of peregrine falcons now breeding in the UK, but just 50 years ago this bird was heading towards extinction.

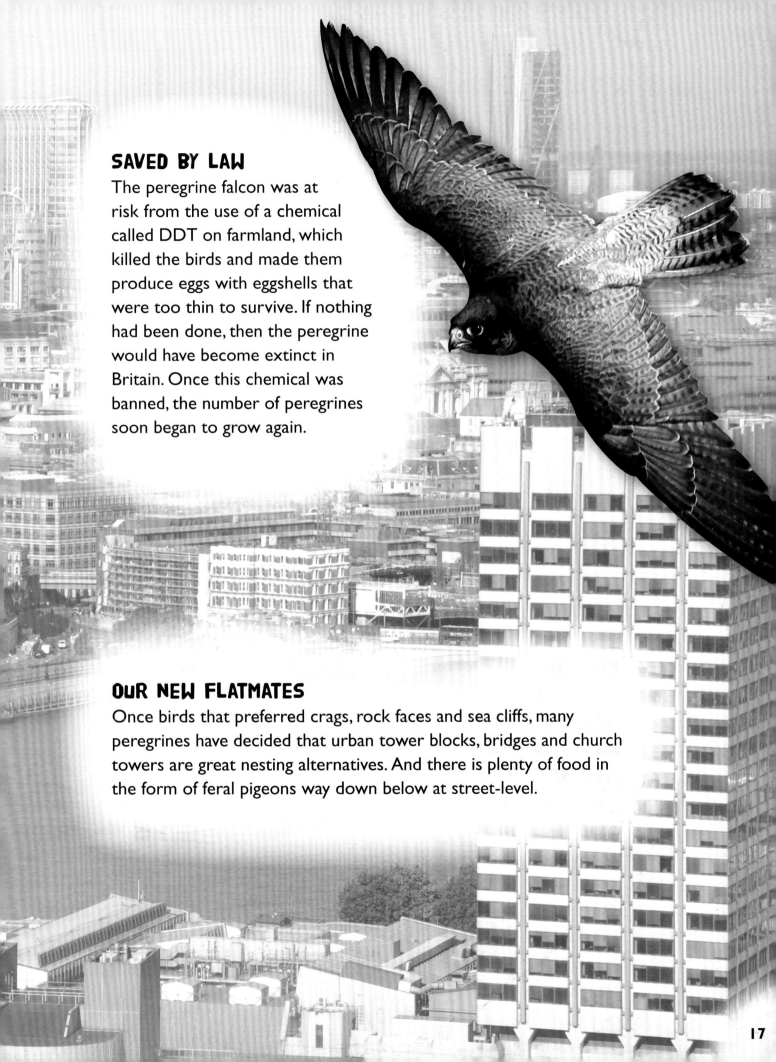

SAVED BY LAW

The peregrine falcon was at risk from the use of a chemical called DDT on farmland, which killed the birds and made them produce eggs with eggshells that were too thin to survive. If nothing had been done, then the peregrine would have become extinct in Britain. Once this chemical was banned, the number of peregrines soon began to grow again.

OUR NEW FLATMATES

Once birds that preferred crags, rock faces and sea cliffs, many peregrines have decided that urban tower blocks, bridges and church towers are great nesting alternatives. And there is plenty of food in the form of feral pigeons way down below at street-level.

SWIFT

Swifts make a quick visit to Britain in the summer. Arriving in towns in early May, their strict insectivorous diet means that by the time insect numbers start to drop off in September, they have already deserted us to spend the winter months in southern Africa.

SWIFT SPOTTING

Look for them nesting in the nooks and crannies under the eaves of buildings. To the nesting swift, there is no difference between these sites and their traditional homes in the crevices of caves or cliffs. Some people confuse them with swallows and martins. Look out for these mini black anchors, as they fly across the sky in small flocks.

Listen out for the noisy screaming call of the swift in high summer too as the young swifts play chasing games with their parents to practise their flying skills.

A swift about to touch down at its nest

Swifts both eat and sleep whilst in the air!

FAB FLIERS

Swifts both eat and sleep on the wing. It is thought that between the time young swifts first leave the nest to when they come back down to earth to breed in their fourth year, these birds will not have landed once during this entire time. Swifts fly a daily average of around 500 miles, as they trawl the skies looking for insects. This means that each adult swift will have probably clocked up over a million miles in its lifetime. As to how many insects they eat, well that is anybody's guess!

HERRING GULL

The distinctive laughing call of the herring gull used to be something only heard on a trip to the seaside, but now you might hear it right across our towns too.

ROOF CLIFFS

It was only in the 1940s that the first herring gulls started using town buildings for nesting. Since then the numbers of urban gulls have shot through the roof! Urban living suits gulls as there are no predators, very little disturbance on rooftops and a large amount of food available nearby.

A VARIED DIET

Like all successful urban invaders, herring gulls are capable of eating most things. In towns, they will clear up the food left out for ducks and swans and expertly rob other birds and people of their lunch. Street lighting also lets them wolf down any discarded takeaways each night before the street-cleaners come along. Out of town rubbish tips are also the perfect place for herring gulls to scavenge for food.

LONG LIVERS

Often mating for life, a pair of herring gulls rear about three chicks a year, which they will defend against all threats, including us humans if we go too close to the nest. Once the young have left the nest, they can live up to the grand old age of 30.

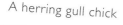
A herring gull chick

URBAN BIRDS

An urban lifestyle is a very popular choice among many of our other feathered friends.

LESSER BLACK-BACKED GULL ▶

You can tell this gull apart from its cousin, the herring gull, by a dark-grey colour across the upper surface of its wings. Lesser black-backed gulls also find town centres the perfect place to bring up their families.

◀ PIED WAGTAIL

Although they will also choose more rural places in which to breed, pied wagtails are attracted by the bright lights of towns and cities during the winter. They like the titbits of food dropped on car parks or pavements. The extra heat pumped out by town buildings also means there are warm places for these gorgeous birds to huddle together overnight until breakfast the following morning.

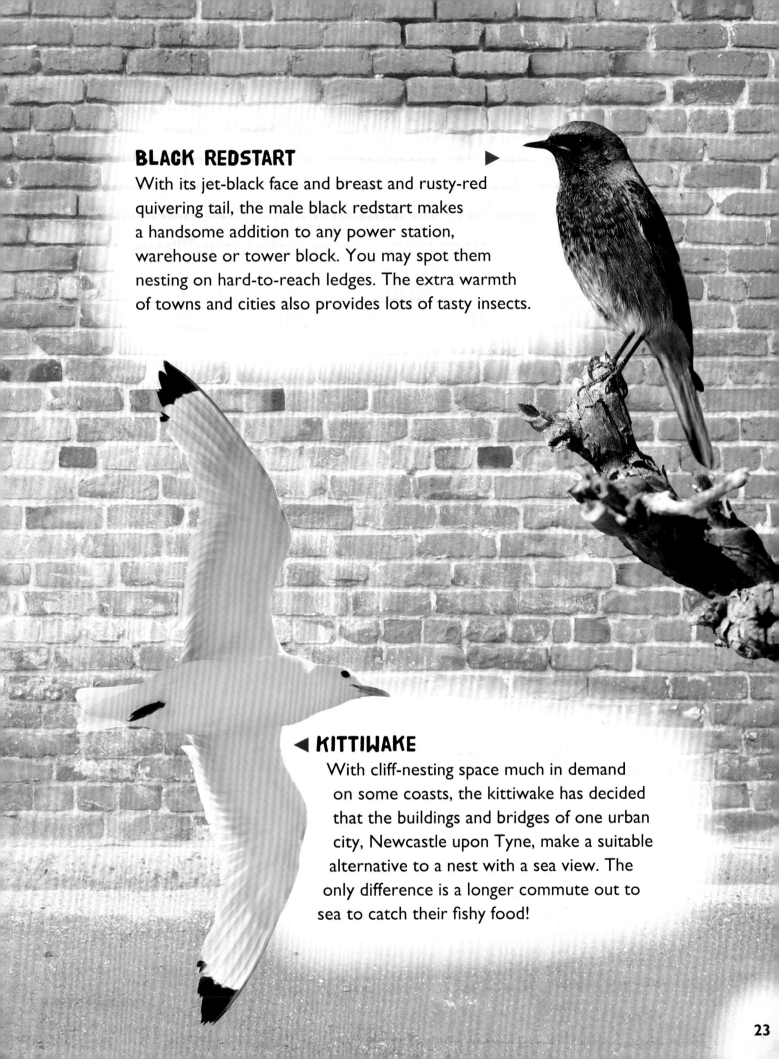

BLACK REDSTART ▶

With its jet-black face and breast and rusty-red
quivering tail, the male black redstart makes
a handsome addition to any power station,
warehouse or tower block. You may spot them
nesting on hard-to-reach ledges. The extra warmth
of towns and cities also provides lots of tasty insects.

◀ KITTIWAKE

With cliff-nesting space much in demand
on some coasts, the kittiwake has decided
that the buildings and bridges of one urban
city, Newcastle upon Tyne, make a suitable
alternative to a nest with a sea view. The
only difference is a longer commute out to
sea to catch their fishy food!

URBAN PLANTS

Look around and you'll find town centres are much greener than you think they are.

LONDON PLANE ▶

You'll find this tree in many cities and towns. Thanks to its constantly shedding bark, thick leathery leaves and the ability of its roots to grow under pavements, the London plane can withstand a lot of urban pollution. It brings a little bit of countryside to even the busiest streets.

◀ ### BUDDLEIA

Since the 'butterfly bush' was first introduced from China in the 1890s, it has relentlessly spread across Britain. Thanks to its light and winged seeds, buddleia has been able to colonise everything from waste ground to walls. This means it often also attracts a range of butterflies into our towns, that are keen to feed on its honey-scented flower spikes.

ROSEBAY WILLOWHERB ▶

Originally a woodland plant, rosebay willowherb first appeared in war-torn London when the plant sprung up from the rubble created by bombing raids in World War II. This gave it the nick-name 'bombweed'. Its light, downy seeds have allowed it to colonise everything from car-parks to cracks in chimneys.

◀ RED VALERIAN

First introduced to our gardens from the Mediterranean 400 years ago, this plant has since hopped over the garden wall and spread into every town in southern and western Britain. Sprouting from rocks and old walls, with white or red flowers, it has quickly become a common and colourful urban summer sight.

THE URBAN GRASSLANDS: GREEN SPACES

Even in the very heart of towns you will find green spaces, sometimes in the most unexpected places. Large areas of our towns are planned to allow for parks, playing fields and gardens. This means that many countryside animals and plants can now choose a home with an urban postcode instead.

RABBIT

The rabbit seems so at home here that it is amazing to think a thousand years ago, Britain was a bunny-free zone! Rabbits were first brought over to Britain by the conquering Normans for food and the use of their fur. They soon spread across the grasslands and right up to the edges of our towns.

ULTIMATE VEGETARIANS

Rabbits are the ultimate vegetarians, nibbling away at a huge variety of different plants. They can be a nuisance to farmers growing crops and to gardeners growing prized flowers. Rabbits are a favourite food for many other animals too but they are helped by good eyesight, an excellent sense of smell and fantastic hearing! They also rarely dine out far from the safety of their underground warren and dash back for cover at the slightest hint of danger.

LOOK BEFORE YOU LEAP

Fond of living under hedges, rabbits are as happy feeding along the roadside verges as in a farmer's field. But they are not very streetwise, so it is unlikely they'll make it to the very centres of our towns any time soon.

KESTREL

This bird of prey is best known for its amazing ability to hover in mid-air while waiting for dinner to turn up in the grasslands below. Kestrels can be found anywhere that provides a home to their favourite food of voles, mice and shrews. The best places to look out for them in the town are above busy roads or railway embankments.

AN URBAN NEST

In the countryside, kestrels tend to rear their young in old tree holes or nests made by other birds. But urban kestrels have decided the artificial 'cliff-ledges' provided by many city tower blocks – or even big nest-boxes – will do the job just as well.

CLUMSY CHICKS

With his grey head and tail, the handsome male cuts a dashing figure as he ferries back and forth with lots of 'furry food' for the young chicks. Despite growing quickly on this rich diet, the chicks still need their parents' help for well over a month after they first leave the nest. These chicks are born clumsy and clueless so it takes time before they are able to hover as well as their parents.

Kestrel chicks need to master the art of hovering before they can catch dinner

STARLING

The starling used to live in town centres and suburbs in much bigger numbers, but it can still be spotted strutting around garden lawns, playing fields and local urban parks. Look for it using its beak to probe for insect larvae, earthworms and spiders.

A BIRD OF MANY COLOURS

From a distance, starlings seem to be sooty black. It is not until you get close up that you can appreciate how stunning these busy little birds are. The breeding plumage of the males has a glossy purple and green sheen, making them dazzle on a sunny day.

Starlings are very sociable birds

BIRD AT RISK

Once breeding is over for the year, starlings become far more sociable, often choosing to eat and sleep together for protection and warmth. The huge urban flocks, however, which were once a common sight in many of our town centres at night, now seem to have mostly disappeared.

Let's hope the sight and sound of a starling flapping its wings while singing its strange song from our rooftops will be an urban spectacle we enjoy for many years to come.

BLACK-HEADED GULL

Despite their name, the heads of these gulls are actually more dark chocolate in colour than black. This 'hood' can only be seen during the short breeding season. For the rest of the year, their heads are mostly white with a dark smudge on either side.

SNATCH AND GRAB

Black-headed gulls are the smallest of all urban gulls and also the ones most likely to visit garden tables or local parks. Look out for them diving down to grab any bits of left out food, or devouring the leftovers from a picnic, often snatching it without even landing. Their table manners leave much to be desired as they squabble over the pickings!

THE WINTER GUEST

Unlike herring and lesser black-backed gulls, black-headed gulls don't breed in towns. Instead, they choose to nest in large, noisy colonies on coastal marshes or flooded gravel pits. During the winter, they flock back to our towns, attracted by the extra warmth and the abundance of free food on offer. They scrounge food by day, and at dusk they fly off to a nearby reservoir or lake to spend the night there and to digest their ill-gotten gains.

Starlings in flight
Let's hope spectacles like this can be seen for years to come.

GRASSLAND PLANTS

With their light seeds and tough nature, some plants are capable of growing any time, any place and anywhere!

DANDELION

This plant is easily recognisable in spring by its yellow flower heads and jagged leaves. Dandelions are able to conquer every nook and cranny of our towns and cities here due to the dandelion's 'clock', which develops in early summer. It only takes a puff of wind for the tiny parachute seeds to take to the air and be carried away, and then only a crack in the pavement for the seed to settle and put down roots.

▼

A dandelion 'clock'

DAISY ▶

The flowers on this plant open only on warm or sunny days and close in the evening. It's easy to see how 'day's eye' eventually became 'daisy'. Flowering from early spring to late summer, this low-growing plant is a bright addition to roadside verges, lawns, local parks or scraps of grass in the hearts of our towns and cities. Daisies flourish in areas where other plants do not cope with being regularly mown or trampled underfoot.

White clover

WHITE AND RED CLOVER ▲

The clovers are famous for their 'trefoil', or three-part leaves. Four-leaf clovers are rare and thought to be a lucky charm. Both white and red clovers can be found along grassy roadsides and in parks. The flowers produce nectar for urban insects in need of a drink during the long, hot summer.

GRASSLAND PLANTS

HOGWEED

This plant gets its name because the flowers supposedly smell of pigs! It flowers every two years and can reach up to two metres in height. The huge flat flower heads are a magnet for all types of insects during the summer months. Often found on roadsides, it will also grow in any urban grassy corner that is left undisturbed.

▼

DANISH SCURVY GRASS

These plants were originally found near the coast. But our habit of spraying salt on roads over the winter has meant this plant now finds these salty urban conditions perfect. This dainty springtime flower has spread like wildfire along roadsides in Britain and can now be found in the very centre of our towns.

SHEPHERD'S PURSE

The name of 'shepherd's purse' comes from the small heart-shaped seed pods which look like the small leather pouches once carried by shepherds. This weed can grow anywhere, from gardens and roadsides to waste places, and is able to flower in almost any month.

GRASSLAND INSECTS

Even the smallest or most unexpected patches of grassland will attract a whole variety of insects into our town centres.

MEADOW BROWN ▶

As its name suggests, this mostly brown butterfly is usually found in meadows. But the meadow brown is also just as happy in patches of urban wasteland, as long as there are lots of different types of grasses on which the females can lay their eggs. Once hatched, the hairy caterpillars will then have plenty of food to nibble, before they eventually transform into butterflies the following summer.

◀ BLACK GARDEN ANT

Like all ants, the black garden ant lives in colonies made up of an egg-laying queen and hundreds of workers. But it is also the most urban of ants, often nesting under stones or paths in gardens or paving slabs in towns. On some warm evenings in summer, lots of winged males and queens take to the air to form new colonies. These swarms also provide a feast for house sparrows and starlings.

COMMON CRANEFLY ▶

You may also know these as 'daddy-long legs'. These huge, long-legged flies are most noticeable when they are attracted to the bright lights of houses and towns in late summer. For most of the year they are squelchy grey grubs, called leatherjackets, which live on the roots of the grasses growing in lawns or along roadsides. Although many people dislike them, the adults are completely harmless and only live for a very short time.

BUMBLEBEES ▶

The warmth in towns and cities makes them attractive places for bumblebees, providing there are plenty of flowers to ensure there is nectar and pollen for them to feed on. There are lots of different kinds of bumblebees. They can be identified by the colour and position of their patterns and stripes.

THE URBAN WETLANDS: RIVERS, LAKES AND CANALS

Nearly every town in Britain has been built around a river or canal. These waterways were once used for transporting goods and people. For the few towns without a waterway, the presence of a few lakes or ponds will also encourage water wildlife to exchange rural living for an urban lifestyle.

OTTER

An otter in the centre of town… surely you can't be serious? 20 years ago, this would have been very remarkable indeed but these days otters are flooding back to urban rivers.

BACK IN OUR WATERS

Otters were widespread in Britain in the 1950s, but the population fell due to pollution from farm pesticides, the disappearance of habitat suitable for rearing their cubs, and hunting with hounds. They disappeared so quickly that by the late 1970s they were almost declared extinct in England. However, a ban on the pesticides, a national cleanup of our waterways and also their protection by law has seen them returning to every county in England.

A HARD SPOT

It might seem that urban living would not suit such a shy and mostly solitary mammal. However, otters have seized the opportunity to live in waterways that contain lots of fish and plenty of places for shelter. Town otters often spend the day in an underground den (or holt), and come out at night. This means that sightings are still very few and far between. Sometimes the only sign of an otter's presence is its fishy droppings (spraints) deposited on waterside stones or logs.

You might be lucky enough to spot an otter early in the morning from a towpath or bridge. Look out for the V-shaped wake through the water created by their head. If they dive for food, keep track of them underwater by the trail of bubbles!

WATER VOLE

The most well known water vole is probably 'Ratty' in Kenneth Grahame's book *Wind in the Willows*. Once a common sight along the edge of any river, canal, pond or lake, the water vole is now in massive decline. In fact it is Britain's fastest disappearing mammal.

VANISHING VOLES

A recent survey showed that the water vole has declined by 94% over the last 50 years. In addition to the usual problems of pollution and the loss of rich bankside vegetation, voles are also preyed on by the American mink. This invader was originally brought over for its fur, and has since both escaped and been released into the wild.

The mink seems desperate to avoid contact with humans, however, which means water voles can still be seen thriving in lakes, rivers and canals in towns.

TOWN LIFE

Water voles live in a system of burrows in the waterside bank, with entrances both above and below water. They are active in the day and can often be seen swimming between vegetation patches as they collect grasses, sedges and roots, which they eat messily on the bankside. Look out for the nibbled remains they leave behind! Let's hope that towns continue to provide a much-needed safe haven for these little vegetarians for many years to come.

A water vole is happiest in water

Water voles have secret exit tunnels

DAUBENTON'S BAT

Also known as the 'water bat', no other species of British bat is so closely linked to large ponds, lakes, canals or slow-moving rivers. Urban buildings and bridges also provide perfect sites for females to rear their babies, so it is no surprise that many Daubenton's have become city slickers!

NIGHT FLIGHTS

Coming out soon after dusk, the Daubenton's bat uses fluttering wing-beats to skim over the water's surface like a mini hovercraft. It snaps up aquatic insects such as mayflies, caddis flies or midges which have just emerged from the water. This bat can also use its tail membrane or its specially adapted large feet to scoop insects from the surface or even just below the water. These catches are then transferred to its mouth mid-flight!

WELL FED

A Daubenton's bat that weighs 7 grams might weigh as much as 11 grams after just an hour of feeding! Daubenton's bats will often patrol the same stretches of water if the feeding is good there. If you shine a torch across the water surface on one of their favoured spots, you can often see them flashing through the beam of light as they go about their business.

This bat is a surface skimmer

A bat lifts itself on those little hooked thumbs

MALLARD

It's easy to recognise a drake mallard. Its glossy, bottle-green head, white neck collar and curly black tail feathers make it one of our most easily identifiable birds.

LUNCH IS SERVED

Another reason mallards are so well known is because they are often seen being fed at our local ponds and lakes. Like all successful 'townies', they will eat everything from leaves and shoots to aquatic insects and small fish. However, it is often bread or grain dropped by us that will have them flocking around your feet for a free lunch.

NESTING NEGOTIATIONS

A female mallard will often lay her brood of between 11 and 14 eggs in a patch of nettles, brambles or long grass. Occasionally, you might also spot them nesting high up on urban buildings in the centres of towns. However, despite the extra safety this urban location gives from predators, it can be a problem when the ducklings are ready to leave the nest.

This female has a typically big brood

AN URBAN TREK

Ducklings are very light, so as long as they are not jumping out of the nest from too high up, they will usually bounce when they hit the pavement. The more difficult task is for the mother to lead them safely to the nearest water. During spring, look out for town traffic either swerving or stopping to avoid the nesting female mallard, as she makes a beeline across busy streets with her ducklings in tow.

KINGFISHER

A flash of electric blue downstream, followed by a dash of orange back upstream can only mean one thing – the river running through your town is home to a kingfisher! No bigger than a sparrow, with a large head and a long dagger-like bill, the kingfisher is one of the jewels in the crown of Britain's rich and varied urban wildlife.

LIVING REQUIREMENTS

This expert fisherman cannot survive without a plentiful supply of bullheads, minnows, loaches and sticklebacks. Therefore a clean water source well stocked with small fish is a necessity. Urban rivers, canals and streams are now cleaner than ever before; this means that kingfishers are a surprisingly regular occurrence in town centres.

A SAFE BANK

Kingfishers also need vertical banks in which to breed. Once they have dug a tunnel into the bank, the young will be reared in a small nesting chamber set well back from the opening and away from the prying eyes of predators.

A kingfisher's chicks are always hidden out of sight

The kingfisher snatches a fish from the riverbed

DIVING FOR DINNER

Watching kingfishers dive for their dinner is a great wildlife spectacle. Perching motionless on a post or a branch overhanging the water, the bird picks out its target before plunging into the water to grab its chosen fish. It will then take the unlucky fish back to the same perch and whack it a couple of times to stun it. The fish is then turned in the bill before being swallowed headfirst – the last thing a kingfisher wants are any gills or spines stuck in its throat!

COMMON FROG

With many rural ponds having either been filled in or become so heavily polluted, urban and suburban ponds are now incredibly important for the survival of one of our best known amphibians, the common frog.

OUT AND ABOUT

The adult frogs spend almost as much time out of the water as actually in it. When they are out hunting for slugs, snails, beetles and caterpillars on mild, damp nights they will always return to the pond in order to court and mate. Once they emerge out of hibernation from either the bottom of a pond or a damp place on dry land, it is fair to say that all the adult frogs will have only one thing on their mind – making frogspawn!

POND LIFE

At popular ponds, you might see a lot of commotion as the males use a combination of croaking and pushing to ensure they gain access to the females as they arrive at the pond. A male will secure a female in a tight embrace, and then fertilize the eggs as the female releases them. On contact with water, the jelly around each egg swells, producing the familiar-looking frogspawn. With luck, tadpoles will emerge from the frogspawn a couple of weeks after.

Look for frogspawn early in the year

TADPOLE ODDS

It's a tough life being a tadpole. Dragonfly nymphs, water beetles, fish and newts all find them a tasty meal. It is estimated that only 1% will ever make it to the stage where they will transform into adult frogs – and without all the ponds in our gardens and town parks it would be even tougher!

The city kingfisher
An upturned supermarket trolley
can make a great place from
which to spot breakfast!

WATER BIRDS

Our urban ponds and park lakes are a magnet for a whole range of water birds.

MUTE SWAN

With its long graceful S-shaped neck, gorgeous white plumage, pointed tail and orange bill, the mute swan is a striking sight in many parks. As many pairs are very territorial and can live into their twenties, it's possible that this is one of the few bird species you may recognise from year to year. The mute swan is mostly vegetarian and will happily accept scraps of bread from a lunchtime sandwich.

▼

CANADA GOOSE ▶

Originally from North America, the Canada goose is much larger than our native geese and can now be found in almost every town park with a lake or large pond. It is immediately identifiable by its black head and neck with a white chinstrap. Listen for its loud nasal honk as it tells other waterfowl to get out of its way. It's as happy wandering around the park lawns as it is sitting on the water, but its toilet visits can be a hazard if you fancy a picnic down by the water's edge!

GREY HERON ▶

Town ponds and lakes (including garden ponds) that are well stocked with fish can expect a visit from the grey heron – one of Britain's tallest birds. Although it will nest alongside other herons in the tops of trees, it usually prefers to be alone when it's out and about. Look for it standing with its head hunched between its shoulders, just like a grumpy old man. When the heron is hunting, it will often stretch out its neck, as it stands motionless for long periods waiting for prey to come in range of its lethal, stabbing beak. Fish make up the majority of its diet, but it won't turn its beak up at a frog or water vole if they are in the wrong place at the wrong time.

WATER BIRDS

COOT ▶

This dumpy water bird has a jet-black head and white bill, which extends into a distinctive white shield on its forehead. Found on almost all lowland bodies of water in Britain, the coot has become a common fixture in any town park with a reasonably sized lake. They are not strong fliers and are happy foraging out of water. Look out for their huge, lobed feet.

MOORHEN ▼

The moorhen is smaller than the coot, and has a red and yellow beak. It also has ragged white lines along its flanks, and white feathers on the underside of its tail, which it flicks constantly when swimming and walking on dry land. They can be found breeding in town park ponds, rivers or ditches.

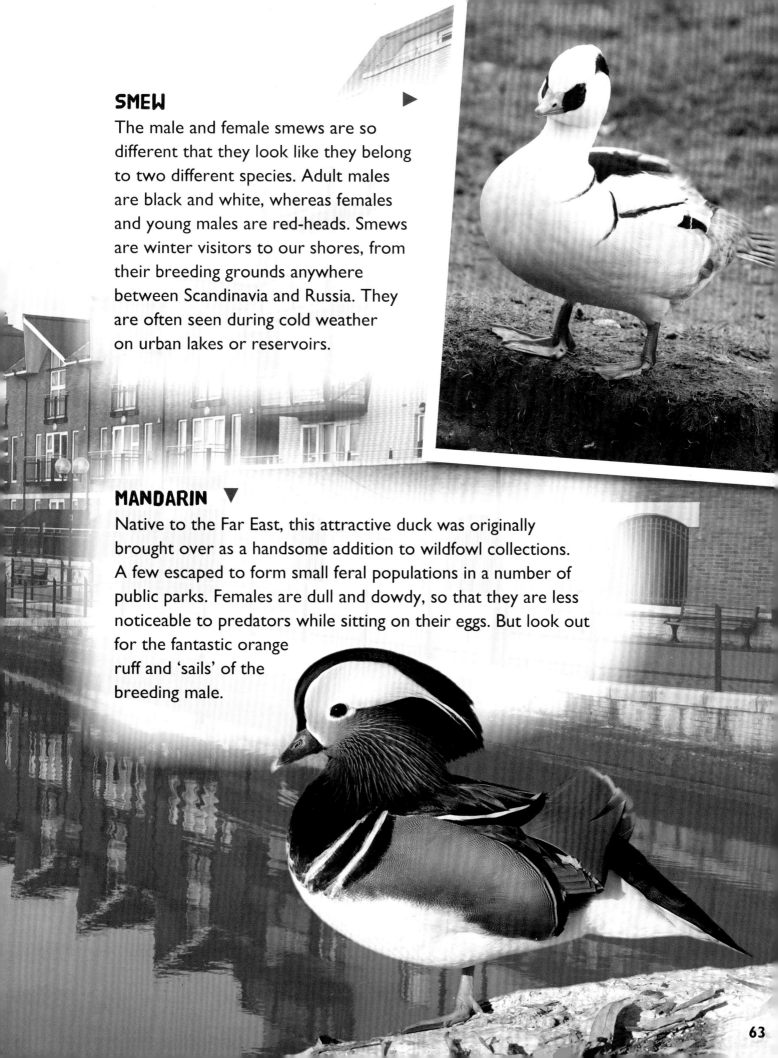

SMEW ▶

The male and female smews are so different that they look like they belong to two different species. Adult males are black and white, whereas females and young males are red-heads. Smews are winter visitors to our shores, from their breeding grounds anywhere between Scandinavia and Russia. They are often seen during cold weather on urban lakes or reservoirs.

MANDARIN ▼

Native to the Far East, this attractive duck was originally brought over as a handsome addition to wildfowl collections. A few escaped to form small feral populations in a number of public parks. Females are dull and dowdy, so that they are less noticeable to predators while sitting on their eggs. But look out for the fantastic orange ruff and 'sails' of the breeding male.

SNAKES, TERRAPINS AND NEWTS

Thanks to the water we provide in our towns, some reptiles and amphibians are now thriving in the most unexpected of places.

RED-EARED TERRAPIN ▶

It is mostly thanks to the *Teenage Mutant Ninja Turtles* TV series from the late 1980s that we now have terrapins living wild in a number of our town ponds and lakes! Originally from North America, they were brought over as pets during the Ninja Turtles craze, but many quickly outgrew their tanks and so were released into local ponds. They are capable of surviving our winters, so they have continued to grow and eat anything from amphibians to fish – even the occasional unfortunate duckling! However, these pond invaders find it hard to breed in Britain's cold climate.

◀ COMMON TOAD

The common toad spends much of its time away from the water. The toads all emerge from their hiding places over a few wet and mild nights in early spring to make their way to their chosen ponds. Nothing will stop the march of the toads as they brave the busy roads, hopefully avoiding any speeding cars.

SMOOTH NEWT

The smooth newt is the most common and widespread of all three of Britain's native newts. You are most likely to encounter one in an urban pond or a ditch with clean water that contain few or no fish. With a spotted chin, flanks and a crest running the length of his body, the male smooth newt is a handsome beast in the breeding season. His underwater courtship involves waving his tail in front of the female's nose.

▼

▼ GRASS SNAKE

Britain's longest snake is rarely found far from the more untouched ponds, ditches and drains in urban locations. As it is an excellent swimmer all our native amphibians, fish and tadpoles figure on its menu. It is totally harmless to humans and its best form of defence if grabbed is to give off a foul-smelling substance, before playing dead!

DRAGONS AND DAMSELS

Dragons and damsels are a common summer sight by even the smallest urban ponds, rivers and canals. These powerful and aerobatic predators are the jet fighters of the insect world.

EMPEROR DRAGONFLY ▶

The emperor is one of Britain's largest dragonflies. Everything about this huge insect is impressive. On warm, sunny days through the summer months, the bright blue and green male can be seen whizzing around with tremendous speed and agility over his chosen territory. This could be anything from a large pond in a park to an urban canal, or even a roadside ditch.

◀ BROAD-BODIED CHASER

Look for the male flying about in early summer, with his broad powder-blue abdomen. The male quickly settles in a suitable garden pond or ditch, and then defends his patch against other rival males. He does this to ensure that any of the yellow-bodied females in his territory will have his undivided attention.

COMMON DARTER ▶

Dividing their time between buzzing around and perching at a favoured spot with a view of its pond, common darters are one of the last dragonflies to emerge in the summer and can often be seen until the first frosts of autumn. The males are bright red, and the females are yellow.

BLUE-TAILED DAMSELFLY

The blue-tailed damsel is found throughout Britain. It may be one of our daintiest damselflies, but it is also one of our toughest because its larvae can tolerate pollution. The showy male is mostly metallic black, but with a single brilliant blue segment close to the end of his abdomen.

▼

FISH

As our urban waterways are now the cleanest they have been in over a century, a range of fish can be seen for the first time from many urban towpaths and town bridges up and down the country.

PIKE ▶

A pike is able to survive in most rivers and ponds with plenty of vegetation. It is a solitary fish that hides in the shadows, waiting for another, unwary fish to drift too close to its duck-like mouth and sharp backward-pointing teeth. This fearsome fish is an indicator of a healthy, unpolluted waterway, making an urban pike both a great find and a very positive sign.

BROWN TROUT ▶

Brown trout spend their entire lives in freshwater, as opposed to their marine cousins which move out to sea before eventually returning as adults. They prefer cold, fast-flowing waters with gravel bottoms, and need plenty of freshwater shrimps and aquatic insect larvae to feed on, so are not found in polluted waters.

ROACH

Like some other successful urban dwellers, the roach has developed an incredibly varied diet, eating anything from aquatic insects to algae. Look out for a roach's orange fins, reddish eyes and silvery sides. They tend to like the company of others, so are most often seen swimming around in shoals. This has given them the nickname of 'water-sheep'.

▲ STICKLEBACK

This is the smallest of all Britain's freshwater fish. The three-spined stickleback can be found anywhere from ditches to rivers. As it is more tolerant of pollution than many other species, it can be found right in our urban heartlands. The stickleback is the only freshwater fish to both build a nest and care for its young during their first few weeks of life.

THE URBAN FORESTS: TOWN TREES

Most towns and cities have busy streets, parks and gardens that are full of trees. Although these were planted for our enjoyment, they have also proved the perfect home from home for many forest-loving animals and plants.

GREY SQUIRREL

This is one of the most frequently seen mammals in British town parks and gardens – apart from humans, of course! The grey squirrel was brought over from the forests of the eastern United States around 130 years ago. It found our countryside so much to its liking that it has spread to almost every corner, apart from little pockets of northern England and the Scottish uplands. Like it or not, the grey squirrel is definitely here to stay.

URBAN ADAPTOR

Grey squirrels will live in parks, gardens or any area with just a few large trees – to which they will escape if they sense danger. Like other successful urban invaders, they have an ability to eat a wide variety of food. In addition to eating nuts, they will also strip tree bark, making them unpopular with foresters!

A squirrel uses a woodpecker's old hole in a tree as a nest

THE ENTERTAINER

Full of character and bold beyond belief, they are fun to watch as they run along slender twigs and leap from tree to tree. Look out for them raiding your bird feeder. The grey squirrel doesn't hibernate, so this is one of the few mammals that you can spot on almost any day of the year.

Grey squirrels steal food from bird feeders

WOOD MOUSE

The wood mouse is the most common of all urban mammals, reaching over a hundred million by the end of each summer! Although its name suggests that this mouse never lives far from woodland, it is equally at home in urban parks and gardens, which give it much-needed cover as it goes about its business.

Wood mice like fruit such as blackberries

AN URBAN RETREAT

Wood mice dig their own burrow, which can be under tree roots or a shed. They will then store food and spend the day here, with the young being born in a small nest chamber lined with leaves and moss. A single female can produce around 20 young between early spring and winter, when wood mice become less active. They have very short lives, with a maximum lifespan of just two years.

Urban wood mice can occasionally be tempted by a discarded sandwich

ON THE GO

The wood mouse can be recognised by its sandy-brown coat, a long tail and large eyes and ears. However, it only comes out to feed at night when it is less likely to be spotted by hungry predators. The wood mouse is sometimes more like a mini kangaroo than a mouse. It hops and bounds around on its large hind feet on the hunt for seeds, fruits, nuts, and the occasional insect.

NOCTULE BAT

The noctule is one of Britain's largest bats. This lean, mean flying machine can commonly be seen on summer nights, whizzing over urban parks in the relentless pursuit of dinner.

BAT SPEED

With a wingspan of over 30cm, the noctule bat is a powerful and expert flyer. Often seen flying high in long, straight lines before dusk, this high speed bat will then swoop down to catch anything from a May bug to a hawk-moth. Food is caught in the mouth or by the tail membrane between its legs, which acts as a pouch.

Noctule bats sleep in holes in trees

BAT LIFE

Noctule bats need holes in large, mature trees to roost in during the day and raise their young. In the summer, females gather together at special nursery roosts to give birth to a single baby. Occasionally, a mother will have twins. Brought up on a rich diet of insects, the young are fully independent of their mother in just a couple of months. They must then eat as much as possible to ensure they will survive the winter months in hibernation, before emerging again the following spring. As they have few predators, noctule bats will probably live to at least the grand old age of ten.

MUNTJAC

Called the 'barking deer' in its native Asia, the muntjac was first introduced into a large estate in Bedfordshire just over 100 years ago. Since then, it has escaped and begun to spread across England and Wales. Originally, it kept to the safety of woods, but it is now increasingly spotted in gardens and on the edges of towns with good cover.

SMALL DEER

The first thing you notice about muntjac deer is how small they are – barely larger than a medium-sized dog. Active during both day and night, the best time to see them is at dawn and dusk when they come out to graze on everything from brambles and tree-bark to shrubs and shoots. The male (buck) grows a short set of antlers each summer. However, it is his fang-like teeth which he uses as a weapon to fight other bucks for the right to mate with a female (doe).

Unlike all other British deer, there is no fixed breeding season, meaning births can occur in any month of the year. After they have given birth, the does are capable of having another fawn just seven or eight months later.

A muntjac fawn will stay close to its mother

TAWNY OWL

As the tawny owl only comes out at night, it is usually far more likely to be heard than seen. Listen out for it in gardens, urban parks and churchyards, as it proclaims its territory and calls to its mate throughout autumn and winter.

THE URBAN TAWNY OWL

Providing there are enough mature trees to roost in and large holes in which to raise a brood, then it seems the tawny owl is happy in towns and cities. In rural woodlands, tawny owls mostly catch voles, mice and shrews, but in a city or town, 'tawnies' seem to favour feathers as much as fur, catching starlings, finches and sparrows and even the odd careless squirrel or brown rat.

OWL FAMILIES

Tawny owl nesting begins in very early spring, with the clutch of two or three eggs hatching a month later. During this time, the owls defend the nest aggressively and the male will even attack humans who come too close! Emerging from the nest-hole a month later, the grey and fluffy young will be dependent on their parents for much of the summer, as they slowly learn the art of flying silently through the trees and catching dinner.

With a night's hunting ahead, tawny owls take it easy during the day.

IVY

Ivy is evergreen, which means it adds a splash of green to our towns and cities during even the coldest and darkest of winters. Ivy is amazingly good at clinging to and scrambling up everything, from trees to gravestones and even people's houses!

LOOK TO THE LEAVES

You can find ivy everywhere, apart from the very north of Scotland. Look carefully at the shape of its leaves. When it is climbing, the leaves are in the recognisable five-lobed shape, but as they reach the top of whatever the plant is climbing they become oval, as the ivy suddenly begins to produce masses of flowers in the sunlight.

When left alone, ivy can even cover whole houses

You can find ivy nearly everywhere

LATE BLOOMER

As it doesn't flower until the autumn, ivy provides a much needed late 'hit' of pollen and sugary nectar for bumblebees, so they can top up their winter stores before hibernation. These flowers will then turn into dark berries, which will help to keep hungry blackbirds and song thrushes fed at the end of winter. Many insects find shelter in the nooks and crannies created by its twisted stems.

Beady-eyed bird
Catching up with tawny owls
during the day is never easy.
The chances are that they will
have spotted you though!

WOODLAND BIRDS

Even though the traditional homes of many birds are in woodland, it hasn't stopped them from using urban trees to help them make a life in towns and cities.

Robins eat worms, seeds and fruit

ROBIN ▶

This symbol of Christmas is one of the few birds which will sing almost all year round, as it defends its territory right the way through the winter. Sometimes, the robin can even be heard in the dead of night in town centres, when it is tricked by a lit streetlight into thinking that dawn is on its way.

WREN ▶

The wren is the little bird with the big voice. A mouse-like bird, with a busy nature, the wren is easily recognised by its small size and cocked tail as it hops around in the dense undergrowth of gardens and urban parks. Wrens mark their territory with a shrill song. The males will then make a number of domed nests, leaving the female to choose the best-hidden location in which to lay her eggs.

◀ BLACKBIRD

Although it is a woodland bird, the blackbird will often be found in town parks and hedgerows. A quarter of all blackbirds now live in our towns and villages. In spring, look for male blackbirds with their black feathers and yellow beaks, singing their song from roofs or television aerials.

WOODLAND BIRDS

JAY

Able to eat everything from acorns to birds' eggs, the jay can now be found in many urban gardens, cemeteries and other places with old, mature trees. Listen out for the jay's harsh screech in your garden or local park, and watch for the flash of white on its rump as it flies.

▼

GREAT SPOTTED WOODPECKER ▶

This is the most common woodpecker in Britain. Great spotted woodpeckers can be seen where there are trees large enough to support their nest-holes. Mostly black and white, the 'great spot' is now a common visitor to garden bird feeders, scattering all the smaller birds as it swoops down to pick up the peanuts. Listen out for it drumming on trees in early spring, and for its loud 'tchick!' call as it warns other birds that this is its patch.

GOLDCREST

The goldcrest is Britain's smallest bird. It weighs just five grams! Look for the bright yellow patch on the male's head. The goldcrest is usually found in conifer woods, but it seems there are also more than enough spiders, flies, small beetles and caterpillars in city gardens and churchyards to keep them alive all winter. On very cold nights, these tiny birds will huddle together to keep warm.

▼

The goldcrest: Britain's smallest bird!

THE URBAN SCRUB: FORGOTTEN CORNERS

Every town has forgotten corners where plants are able to grow without the threat of either being chopped back or cut down. These places can become an impenetrable mass of thorns and stings due to brambles and nettles. If they are left alone for long enough, they will become an important oasis for all kinds of wildlife.

BANK VOLE

How do you tell the difference between a mouse and a vole? Small ears and eyes, a blunt nose and a short tail will tell you that the small mammal you are looking at is a vole. The bank vole is much more ginger in colour and far fonder of scrub than the more rural field vole. The field vole is also unsurprisingly usually found in fields! Bank voles are found in woodlands and hedgerows.

OUT IN THE DAYTIME

The bank vole is much more likely to be seen during the daylight than a mouse. Rarely found far from bramble thickets, hedgerows and woody scrub, the bank vole often builds an underground nest lined with dried grass. Around this nest, the vole will then create burrows and surface tunnels, along which it scurries to find shoots, leaves, berries and nuts to eat.

Bank voles nesting

NIMBLE CLIMBER

The bank vole is a nimble climber and can be seen clambering through bramble patches as it searches for blackberries. But life is tough for a vole. Even those that avoid the jaws of a weasel, the paws of a cat or the talons of a tawny owl will rarely live more than 18 months.

Bank voles have to look out for predators

SLOW WORM

**Although it is often mistaken for a snake,
the slow worm is in fact a legless lizard!
Slow worms make a living by squeezing
into small gaps to shelter or find food.**

THE HIDER

The slow worm is a harmless and very secretive animal. It is rarely seen
out during the day for fear of being caught by everything from cats and
rats to kestrels. Like all reptiles, it loves the heat. When the sun is out, it
will often hide under a flat stone or piece of discarded metal sheeting,
absorbing the warmth. It is only when dusk falls and the coast is clear,
that it will then come out to track down its favourite food… slugs!

A PEACEFUL LIFE

The slow worm emerges from hibernation in March to mate, but its wriggling young will not be born until early autumn. Sunny, scrubby and undisturbed areas in our parks, gardens and railways provide the perfect homes for these creatures. If left in peace, they can live a long time. One slow worm in captivity even reached the grand old age of 50!

A slow worm on the lookout for slugs

COMMON LIZARD

Your first sight of a common lizard may be that of its tail disappearing out of view. It was probably basking in the sun seconds before. The scrub-covered banks and wastelands found in many towns and cities can be the perfect places to spot these handsome and lively reptiles as they go about their daily business.

SUN WORSHIPPERS

When they awake from hibernation in early spring, the common lizards spend a lot of their time basking in the sun. Once warm, they use their excellent eyesight and agility to catch a whole range of insects and spiders. A mature male has bright yellow or orange underparts, which he uses to court the female lizards. If the female is impressed, they will mate. She will give birth to between five and eight tiny lizards about three months later.

A common lizard is a dedicated sun worshipper

AN ESCAPE TAIL

Despite being extremely active and alert creatures, common lizards still fall prey to cats, rats and birds. However, they do have one very clever trick up their sleeve to avoid being eaten. If a predator seizes its tail, the lizard can shed it instantly. While the still-wriggling tail provides a diversion, the lizard is free to escape!

COMMON SHREW

Common shrews are heard more often than they are seen. The common shrew spends most of its life being both fiercely territorial and solitary. When two shrews meet, they will often scream at each other with shrill squeaks. In shrew language this means "back off!"

TINY MEAT-EATERS

A common shrew is smaller than a house mouse and can be identified by a long pointed nose, tiny eyes and small rounded ears. Active during both day and night, the shrew is constantly on the move as it bustles around using its super-flexible nose and sensitive whiskers to forage for food in the soil and leaf-litter. The common shrew is a meat-eater and will devour anything from woodlice and spiders to slugs and insects. If they go without food for just a few hours they could die of starvation.

VERY COMMON SHREWS

Common shrews are found throughout most of Britain and can live in most places that have thick cover. In many towns dense grass and scrub that have been left to grow wild will probably be home to a number of these fierce little predators.

Common shrews are always on the lookout for food

Green city
Given half a chance, wildlife will reclaim any forgotten urban corner.

SCRUB BIRDS

Urban scrub provides a safe place for many birds to nest and also plenty of food to feed a family of hungry chicks.

BLACKCAP

This bird is named after the male's black coloured cap. However, contrary to their name, the female and young male's cap is actually reddish-brown! The blackcap is a visitor to Britain from the Mediterranean. It comes here to breed in the summer. Recently a number of blackcaps which normally spend their summers in Germany and Austria have also started to come to Britain for the winter. This means the blackcap can now be seen here all year round.

Blackcaps are fond of copses, thickets and bushes. Large urban parks or gardens are the best places to hear the male's sweet and melodic song in spring. Their young are fed on caterpillars, flies and beetles, but in the winter blackcaps will be more than happy living off anything from ivy berries to bits of bread.

Male blackcaps have a very tuneful song

WHITETHROAT

Whitethroats visit Britain from northern Africa for just a few brief summer months. They seek out bushy areas to raise their young before making their long return journey back to Africa. Look for them with their long tails and white throats, as they sing their short scratchy song from the top of a road or rail-side bramble patch.

It is the male who takes responsibility for 'house building'. He makes several cup-shaped nests low down in scrub, from which the female chooses one. Once the eggs have hatched, both male and female will then scour the surrounding vegetation for beetles, aphids, caterpillars and flies to feed their chicks. A pre-migration meal of blackberries ensures they don't run out of fuel on their way back to Africa!

SCRuB PLANTS

Scrub contains some of our most familiar wild plants. These, in turn, provide a free bed and breakfast service for a whole range of wildlife.

▲

SILVER BIRCH

This tree is immediately recognisable by its silvery bark with black cracks. Birch may not be one of Britain's largest native trees, but it is certainly one of the fastest growing. It produces huge numbers of seeds, which are then blown about like dust in the wind. Silver birch is often one of the first trees to begin turning forgotten areas of scrub back into woodland.

BRAMBLE ▶

There can hardly be a patch of scrub in the land that is not home to this prickly, but fruity, plant. Known for its blackberries in late summer, bramble also produces the most wonderful show of blossom, which makes a great nectar supply for a whole range of insects. With its spiky stems climbing through and over anything in its way, it also provides protection for everything from nesting birds to hibernating hedgehogs – making it a fantastic plant for wildlife.

◀ NETTLE

Familiar to anyone who has had a painful brush against this plant, the nettle is well-defended by its stinging hairs. 'Stingers' can be found in any waste place, especially around old buildings or roadsides. Young nettle shoots are actually very tasty, and can be eaten like spinach, or made into soup. But older stinging nettles are best avoided!

SCRUB PLANTS

Cities and towns are full of alien invaders too – plants that didn't originally grow here.

JAPANESE KNOTWEED

This plant was first introduced to Britain's gardens from the Far East. However, Japanese knotweed promptly 'hopped' over the fence and has now spread to every corner of the country. Japanese knotweed is able to sprout from the smallest root fragment which means it is even capable of growing through tarmac! This urban invader can be found taking over anywhere from car parks to urban allotments. ▼

OXFORD RAGWORT

Originally collected from the volcanic slopes of Mount Etna in Italy, Oxford ragwort was first planted within the walls of the Oxford University Botanic Garden. It wasn't long before its light and downy seeds wafted out of the garden and reached the railway station. Railway sidings offer similar conditions to its volcanic home. The plant began to spread around Britain, as its seeds were sucked along and spread by passing trains. Oxford ragwort can now often be seen sticking out of factory walls, along motorway verges and on building sites.

PINEAPPLEWEED

From its original home in north-east Asia, this low-growing plant can often be seen on roadsides and in waste places. It has now spread all over the world. Its seeds are thought to have hitched a ride in the treads of car tyres (carried by mud). Pineappleweed is tough and can survive a lot of trampling for a little plant. If crushed, it smells strongly of pineapple.

SCRUB BUTTERFLIES

You don't have to be in the middle of the countryside to spot a surprising variety of butterflies. A little scrub is all some of these 'flutter-bys' need to thrive in our towns and cities.

HOLLY BLUE ▶

If you see a small flash of blue flitting around your gardens or town centre, then you've probably spotted a holly blue butterfly. Unlike other blue butterflies in Britain, which rarely stray far from grassland, the holly blue would much rather hang around shrubs and scrubland. The males are also quite happy to roam over large distances as they search for food and females.

Holly blues are seen on the wing in spring and summer. Their favourite plants for egg-laying are holly in the spring and ivy in the summer. Look for them sitting on leaves, as they fidget with their wings firmly closed. They rarely rest for long. It only takes a splash of sunshine and they're off again, flying high above the bushes and beyond.

Black spots underneath a holly blue's wings

GATEKEEPER

The gatekeeper is a butterfly that likes hot weather. It doesn't emerge until high summer and then only makes an appearance on warm, sunny days. It lives in colonies in southern Britain. The gatekeeper also needs quiet sheltered corners, where the grass is left uncut and plants like bramble are allowed to blossom.

It's easy to tell a sunbathing male gatekeeper from a female, as the males are both smaller and have a broad black band across their forewings.

▼

THE URBAN CAVES: HOMES AND BUILDINGS

Living alongside humans can offer a number of advantages to a variety of wildlife. These animals don't just think of our homes, shops, offices and factories as the places designed for us to live in and work. They are often warm, mostly free of predators and have plenty of food going spare. Which means they offer everything that mammals, birds and invertebrates need too!

HOUSE MOUSE

The house mouse was accidentally brought over from Asia by traders well before the Romans conquered Britain. It has been living under our floorboards and behind our skirting boards ever since. It is able to live in the wild, but it is happiest being in the places where we live and work.

FREQUENT HOUSE GUEST

A small rodent with beady eyes, large ears, and a tail the same length as its body, the house mouse has greyish-brown coloured fur and a very distinctive whiff, smelling strongly of… mouse! House mice thrive where food is stored or processed. Even though grain is their favourite food, they are even capable of making a meal out of a bar of soap when they are hungry! But they also have an unfortunate habit of going to the toilet where they feed.

MOUSE HOUSES

House mice can breed at an astonishing rate. They are capable of producing up to 10 litters a year. Each litter averages between five and seven babies and numbers can quickly explode when there is little disturbance and plenty of food on offer. Due to improvements in our hygiene, the house mouse is not as common as it once was in the modern home. But in large urban buildings where food is either housed or served, colonies of these busy little mice will often be active around the clock.

A house mouse gnaws its way into a night-time meal

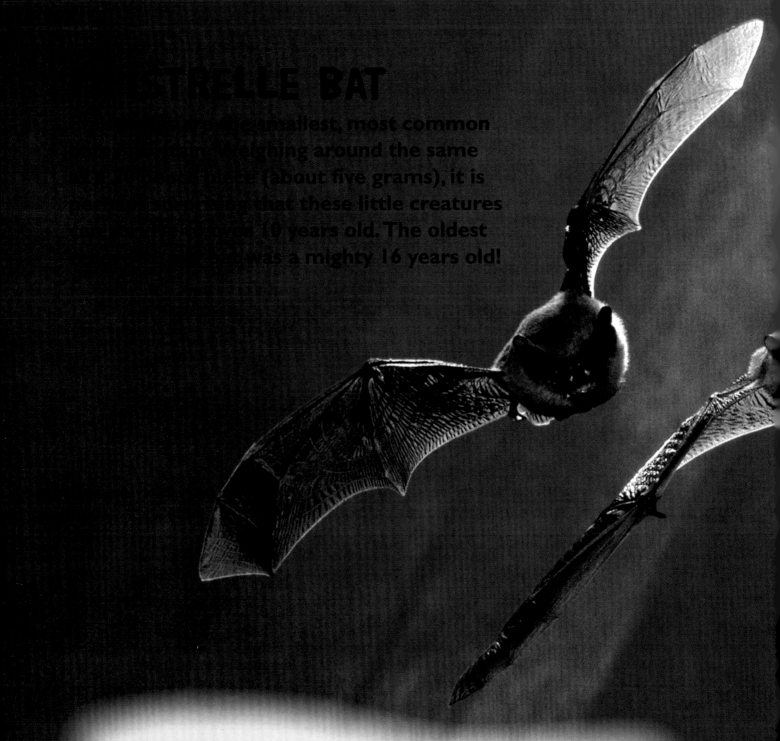

PIPISTRELLE BAT

Pipistrelles are the smallest, most common
British bat. Weighing around the same
as a pound coin (about five grams), it is
perhaps surprising that these little creatures
can live to over 10 years old. The oldest
recorded 'pip' was a mighty 16 years old!

NIGHT FLIT

Despite their tiny body size and weight, their wingspan during
flight will reach over 20 cm. They often emerge well before dusk,
so look for them flitting around parks and gardens before it becomes
too dark for us to see them. Small moths, midges and other insects
are their main source of food. Pipistrelles use sound waves to build
a picture of the world around them and to find food. This feeding
method is so effective that it has been estimated a 'pip' can catch
as many as 3000 insects each night.

ROOF DWELLERS

Roof spaces in our homes appear to be their favourite locations both for hibernating during the winter and rearing their young during the summer. Pipistrelles are protected by law, so if you have a colony living in your roof then you should consider yourself very lucky to have been chosen!

Pipistrelle bats live in this roof

HOUSE SPARROW

The tame, yet wary house sparrow has probably been a part of our lives ever since we first moved out of caves and began living in huts. Despite an alarming decline in recent years, the constant chirping of the house sparrow perched on the guttering is still the sound of the suburbs during summer months.

SPARROW FAMILIES

Male sparrows are immediately recognisable by their grey caps and black bibs. It is also the males who often choose the nest-site – they only need to find the smallest chink in a roof tile to give access to a suitable nesting location. Both male and female will then build the nest, before a clutch of four or five eggs is laid. The adults mostly eat nuts and seeds, but the young are fed on a diet of caterpillars and other insects. This rich food means the chicks are ready to leave the roof after just two weeks. However, the parents will still help them out for another couple of weeks before they then start preparing for their next brood. House sparrows often pair for life.

Grey caps and black bibs show these birds are male

A DROP IN NUMBERS

No-one is sure exactly why the number of house sparrows has dropped so dramatically. But there is no doubt that our town houses would be much duller places without these chatty neighbours to keep us entertained.

HOUSE MARTIN

House martins spend the winter swooping for insects in the African skies. So it is always an exciting moment when the house martins arrive back in our towns to take advantage of the British summer 'bug bonanza'. These birds traditionally build their nests on cliff-sides, but they must have seen little difference between natural rock-faces and the vertical walls of our suburban homes.

WELCOME BACK

Once back, their next job is to find the nearest muddy puddle to collect material for building a new mud-nest or to make repairs to a nest used in previous years. They are smaller than swallows, and their blue-black and white plumage makes them easy to identify. House martins are happiest when airborne, and they only ever land on the ground when gathering nesting material. They are a sociable species and enjoy perching on wires with friends and family in between feeding sessions.

A house martin looking for nesting material

A SUMMER HOME

The house martin's diet consists of flying food in the form of aphids, gnats, beetles, flies and flying ants, which are then presented to the growing chicks as a 'ball' of insects. The hard-working parents will often try to raise a second and even third clutch of chicks while they are here, occasionally helped by their offspring from the first brood. However, by the end of October all house martins will have left for Africa.

A house martin feeding its chicks

JACKDAW

Traditionally, jackdaws were more common in the countryside. However, the smallest member of the crow family has also discovered there is much to be gained by moving into our towns. These clever birds have a constant eye for opportunity, and find chimneys provide the perfect place to rear a brood of chicks. This means they are now a regular fixture on top of town roofs.

TRYING TO HIDE

Despite being wary of humans, the jackdaw often gives away its presence by the loud 'tchack!' call, from which it gets its name. Look for its ash-grey hood, a feature which helps separate the jackdaw from its similar but larger cousins, the rook and carrion crow. Jackdaws feed mostly on the ground, and will eat pretty much anything, from insects to eggs and young birds. They are also much more common on garden bird feeders than you might think, but often arrive and depart well before we get out of bed!

A jackdaw visiting a feeder

CHIMNEY NEST

When building a nest in a chimney, the male drops sticks down until some catch, eventually creating a platform. The young grow slowly and it is often at least five weeks before they are ready to leave the nest. Once they have emerged blinking into the light, they will need help from their parents for several more weeks before they are ready to join the other neighbourhood jackdaws in a flock for the winter.

A jackdaw collecting sticks to make its nest

Lots of ladybirds
Sheds and outhouses make the perfect, safe place for ladybirds to sit out the winter until spring.

HOUSE INSECTS

In summer most insects are out and about in parks and gardens. However, a small number find our homes and outbuildings the perfect sanctuary to see out the winter.

SMALL TORTOISESHELL ▶

Found in many places from sea level to mountaintops, the small tortoiseshell is one of our most common garden visitors to flowers, such as buddleia, during the spring and late summer. After they've had their fill of nectar, the adults will look for somewhere to pass the winter. Often choosing an outhouse or cold room in the house to hibernate, they will then just 'shut up shop' until spring. Once the warmer days come, they will wake up and go back out into the open with just two things on their minds: refuelling and mating!

If you find a hibernating butterfly, try not to disturb it. Waking a butterfly during winter means it will waste fat reserves that are crucial for seeing it through the toughest time of year.

Spot a small tortoiseshell by its striking colours

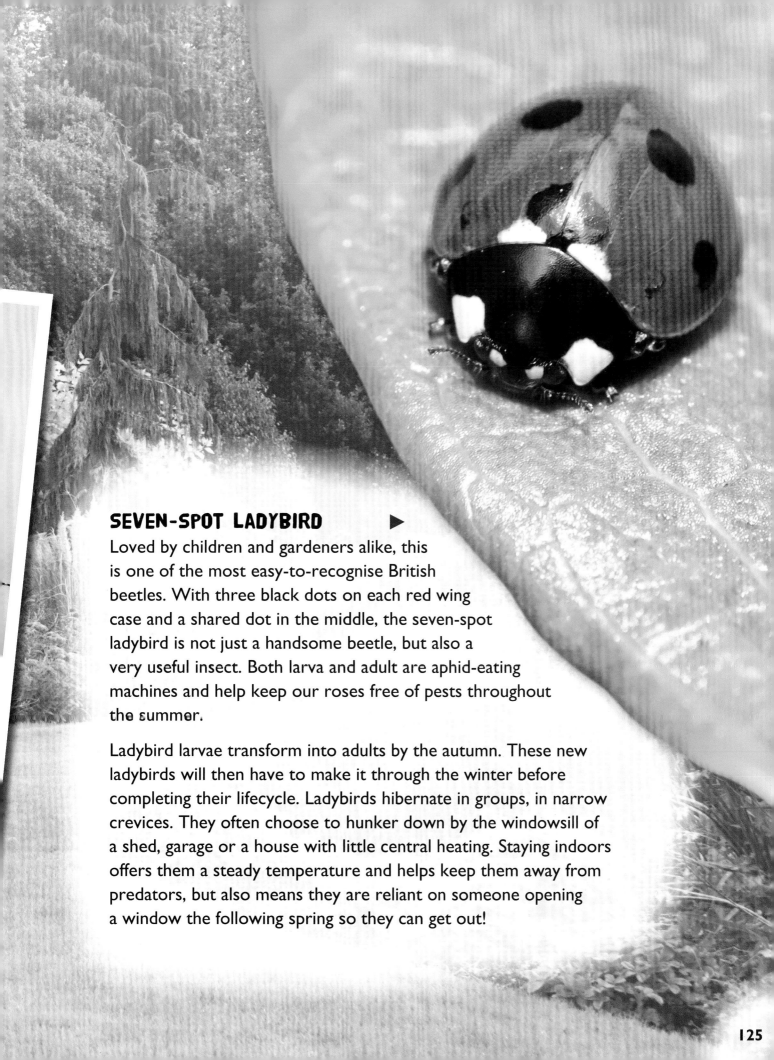

SEVEN-SPOT LADYBIRD ▶

Loved by children and gardeners alike, this
is one of the most easy-to-recognise British
beetles. With three black dots on each red wing
case and a shared dot in the middle, the seven-spot
ladybird is not just a handsome beetle, but also a
very useful insect. Both larva and adult are aphid-eating
machines and help keep our roses free of pests throughout
the summer.

Ladybird larvae transform into adults by the autumn. These new
ladybirds will then have to make it through the winter before
completing their lifecycle. Ladybirds hibernate in groups, in narrow
crevices. They often choose to hunker down by the windowsill of
a shed, garage or a house with little central heating. Staying indoors
offers them a steady temperature and helps keep them away from
predators, but also means they are reliant on someone opening
a window the following spring so they can get out!

HOUSE INSECTS

A number of not-so-welcome house invaders have also made our homes theirs!

SILVERFISH ▶

This bizarre-looking insect is wingless and looks a bit like a tiny silver fish with three tails. Basements, bathrooms, garages, attics and under sinks are exactly the types of moist, damp places that this household pest likes to hide away in during the day. It comes out at night to eat anything from paper and glue to carpets and dandruff! It is harmless to humans and it is also becoming rarer in our dry, centrally-heated houses.

COCKROACH ▶

Of the 4500 different species of cockroaches identified around the world, only a handful has decided to share the places in which we live or work. They are able to exist in virtually any human habitation, but they prefer old buildings with crannies, crevices, hollow walls and warm pipes, and will always run away when exposed to light. As they eat our food and often foul it in the process, cockroaches are generally despised. However, they only exist in places where hygiene levels are poor – so maybe it's us humans who need to clean up our act!

BED BUG ▶

Waking up itching and scratching, with small red rashes on your arms and chest often means only one thing – you have just shared your bed with a nocturnal bloodsucker! No larger than a ladybird, these bugs have recently made a comeback in houses and hotels, and have also been able to hitch-hike around the world in traveller's dirty rucksacks. The key to a bed bug-free house is cleanliness, combined with regular checks to make sure they haven't made an appearance.

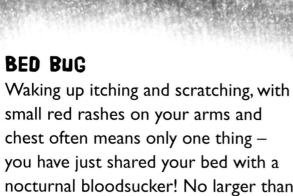

CLOTHES MOTH ▲

These moths are famous for entering our wardrobes and ruining our suits, skirts and sweaters. It is not the moths that do the nibbling but their hungry caterpillars, which will feed on any natural fibres such as cotton, wool, silk and linen. These moths tend to run rather than fly when disturbed.

SPIDERS

Like it or not, spiders are much more common than you might think in the places we choose to live.

HOUSE SPIDER ▶

Often seen on autumn evenings, sprinting across the carpet whilst searching for females, the male house spider is certainly built for running. One of only two or three closely related species, the house spider has hitched a lift around the world in ships, trains and removal vans. Now accustomed to the warmth of our homes and offices, they would be unable to survive outdoors for long.

◀ TUBE WEB SPIDER

The tube web spider first arrived in British ports in the cargo of ships from the Mediterranean. It has since spread to many coastal towns and slowly begun to move inland too. A large spider (at least for Britain), it lurks inside a silk-lined tunnel of a wall crevice and uses silk trap-lines to alert it to any passing prey. When it feels the vibrations from a bug stumbling across the lines, the spider leaps out and pounces on the victim. The bug is killed quickly with a venomous bite and the spider retreats back into the tunnel to digest its meal.

DADDY-LONGLEGS SPIDER ▶

This spider is sometimes also called the 'cellar spider'. Often confined to a tangle of barely visible threads in the corners of the ceiling, the daddy-longlegs spider can look more like a crane fly than a spider. It moves very slowly and uses its long, slender legs to probe the surroundings as it invades other spiders' webs, often eating them in the process!

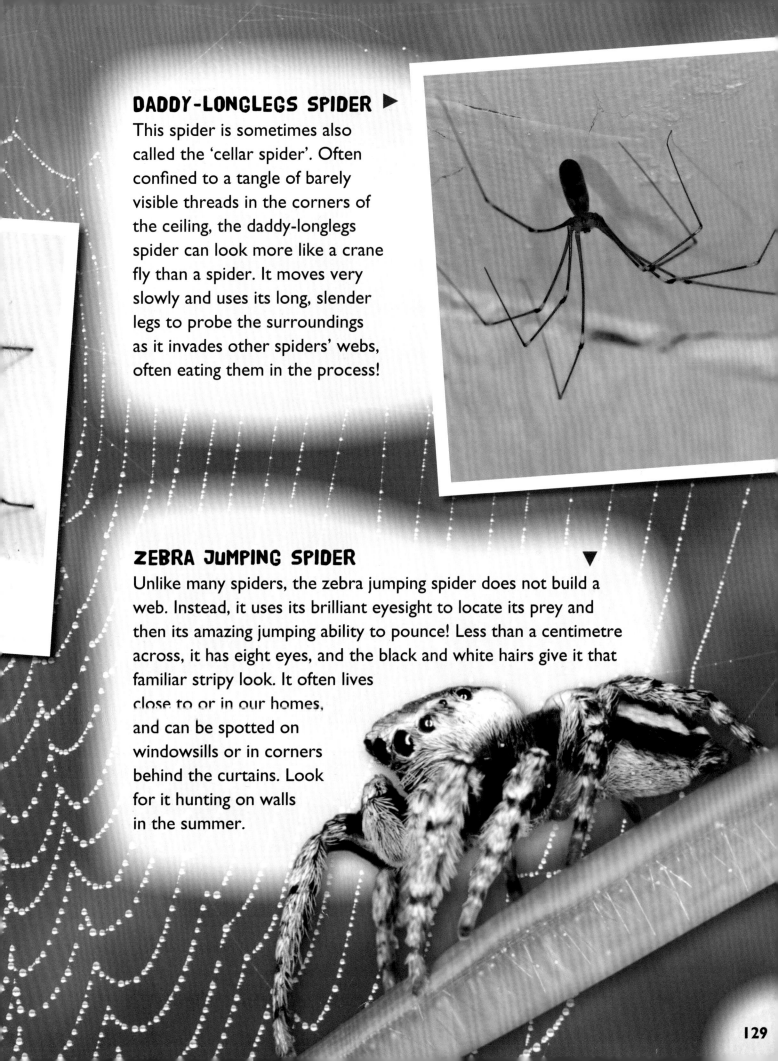

ZEBRA JUMPING SPIDER ▼

Unlike many spiders, the zebra jumping spider does not build a web. Instead, it uses its brilliant eyesight to locate its prey and then its amazing jumping ability to pounce! Less than a centimetre across, it has eight eyes, and the black and white hairs give it that familiar stripy look. It often lives close to or in our homes, and can be spotted on windowsills or in corners behind the curtains. Look for it hunting on walls in the summer.

THE URBAN MOSAIC: A LITTLE BIT OF EVERYTHING

Many urban creatures do not live in just one habitat, but prefer to use a combination of desert, wetland, woodland, scrub, grassland and caves during the course of the year. This means that towns are perfect for these types of animals, as they are full of everything from gardens and parks to scrubland and river banks.

HEDGEHOG

Britain's only spiny mammal has been a familiar creature in gardens, parks and churchyards for centuries. It prefers a mixture of trees, meadows, scrub and hedgerows, and is frequently found along the borders between these different habitats – so really it should be called an 'edge-hog'!

A CREATURE OF MANY TALENTS

The hedgehog usually comes out at dusk and uses a combination of its excellent sense of smell and sensitive whiskers to track down beetles and earthworms. Despite its dumpy appearance, it can climb surprisingly well and can even swim, although that's not its favourite way of getting around! When alarmed, its immediate response is to roll into a ball with its spines sticking out, to help put off predators.

Spines make the perfect armour

HEDGEHOG LIFE

Hedgehogs hibernate through the winter when food is scarce, and emerge in the spring ready to mate. Most young are born in early summer. Their first bristly spines sprout within hours of birth. Unfortunately, any litters born later in the year will often find it difficult to put on enough weight before hibernation, and so rarely make it through the winter. The hedgehog is still a common creature in many towns, but sadly it seems to be declining.

BADGER

The badger is hard to see due to the fact it usually comes out at night, but it often makes visits to our parks and suburban gardens. Instantly recognisable by its black and white face markings, the badger is one of our best-known British mammals.

A DAY UNDERGROUND

Badgers spend most of their day underground in a large burrow system (or sett) which has been dug out with their powerful forepaws and strong claws. These setts are often found under trees, hedgerows or scrub, and consist of a network of tunnels and sleeping chambers. Groups of badgers living together are often related and can number between five and ten different animals.

Badgers visit gardens much more than you think!

Badgers hunt using their incredible sense of smell

FORAGING FOR FOOD

When they come out at dusk, each group looks for food within their own territory, which should provide enough earthworms, beetles and fruit to keep them well fed. When these territories also include gardens, badgers are not shy in helping themselves to any household scraps, or even pet or bird food, that has been left out. They track down their food with a sense of smell that is 800 times better than our own! Badger cubs are born in the depths of winter, and appear above ground for the first time in April or May. Any badgers that avoid meeting an untimely end on our roads could easily live to well over ten years old.

ROE DEER

The beautiful and elegant roe deer has always been an animal that seems happiest in the woodland and farmland of our countryside. However, recently a number have set up home in some of our larger urban parks and cemeteries. You may even spot one in your back garden looking for a tasty shrub or two.

SHORT, SHARP ANTLERS

Roe deer are busiest at dawn and dusk, and are usually seen either on their own or in small groups. The male (or buck) is easily identified by his short, sharp antlers. When the antlers are fully grown in May, he uses them to defend his territory and to fight other bucks for the right to mate with a female (or doe).

DEER KIDS

The female roe deer will not give birth until the following spring. She usually has twins, but just occasionally triplets are born. The spotted baby deer (fawns) are usually hidden away as they are very vulnerable to predators, but can occasionally be seen lying among brambles or long grass. Their mother is always close by and returns to feed them several times a day until they are ready to follow her and feed on shoots and shrubs a few months later.

A roe deer fawn must stay well-hidden

SPARROWHAWK

The sparrowhawk is a predator of small woodland birds, and has become a common fixture in many urban centres where we regularly feed birds. With its broad rounded wings and long tail, the sparrowhawk is an incredible aerial assassin!

SOLITARY BIRDS

Sparrowhawks are secretive and solitary birds. The only time that the males and females are usually seen in the open together is at the start of the breeding season. The female is much larger and almost twice as heavy as the male. This means that despite being less nimble, she can cope without eating for longer periods whilst she is sitting on the eggs. This size difference also means that they tend to catch different prey. The male goes for smaller birds, such as great tits or chaffinches, leaving the female to hunt down blackbirds, starlings and pigeons.

STAYING WITH THE NEST

In a carefully hidden nest, usually built high up in trees such as conifers, the female will stay with the chicks when they are young. During this time, she must depend on her mate to find enough food for both her and their growing chicks. The male will often catch small birds by surprising them, using a garden hedge to hide behind until he is close enough to pounce!

If the sparrowhawk is big, it is likely to be a female

Garden visitor
With plenty of slugs and snails on offer, plus the occasional leftover bowl of cat or dog food, it's no surprise that hedgehogs adore gardens.

LITTLE OWL

No larger than a starling, this little predator needs a combination of old trees in which to nest, and a mixture of open spaces, hedges and copses to provide plenty of places to hunt for food.

THE SCOWLING OWL

The little owl was introduced to southern England from Europe in the 19th century. It spread slowly across lowland England and Wales, only reaching southern Scotland in the last few decades. The black pupils, yellow eyes and strong white 'eyebrows' give the impression that the little owl is always scowling! Most active at dusk and dawn, the little owl will catch and eat everything from small mammals and birds to beetles and earthworms.

Little owl chicks

DEVOTED PARENTS

Little owls like to nest in holes in mature trees, where the female incubates three to four eggs before brooding the chicks. As the chicks grow quickly, both parents start hunting for food in an attempt to keep up with their huge appetites. Even after they've left the nest, they still beg food from their parents for a few more weeks as they learn the tricks of the trade. Once fledged, the young never travel far. It seems that, for a little owl, home is where the heart is!

MAGPIE

From a distance, it's easy to forget what a beautiful bird the magpie is. It is not until you look closer at its dark feathers that you can see the incredible blue-green sheen along its wings and long tail, making this bird dazzle when the sun catches its plumage.

Magpie visiting a bird table

A SAFER PLACE TO LIVE

Over the last 50 years, the magpie has spread from the countryside into towns and cities. Urban living suits the magpie as it can take advantage of the large amount of food we leave around. Also, on farmland it is thought of as a pest and often shot, but it is mostly left alone by town dwellers, leaving it free to raise a family.

BERRIES NOT JEWELS

A magpie is able to eat a lot of things, from fruit and berries to carrion, beetles and even dog poo! It also has a reputation for raiding the nests of other birds for their eggs and chicks. It builds large domed nests in trees or tall shrubs, and lays a clutch of five or six eggs in spring. The idea that magpies steal and keep jewellery and other shiny objects in the nest is now considered a myth. In fact, the only thing that magpies do hide is food, which is often squirreled away during times of plenty to eat later.

With their 'chack-chack' call, magpies are as easy to hear as to see

CITY BIRDS

Lured in by the food we leave out or the natural food readily available in our gardens, many different species of bird are now as happy in our towns as they were in the country.

BLUE TIT

The blue tit is actually a woodland bird, but only needs a few trees and shrubs (or a nestbox) and some food to be encouraged to live in the heart of our towns. Its small size, blue cap, black line through the eye and yellow belly all help tell it apart from its cousin, the great tit.

Blue tits feed their chicks on a protein-rich diet of caterpillars, insects and spiders in the summer, before changing to nuts and berries during the autumn and winter. Each pair of blue tits will usually raise a single clutch of eight to ten chicks every year. Occasionally, this figure can reach as high as 15 or 16!

▼

GREAT TIT

The biggest and bossiest of all the tits, the great tit can immediately be identified by the black stripe running down the centre of its yellow breast and belly. Its 'teacher–teacher' call is a common sound in our parks and gardens, which the male uses to attract a female and make sure other male great tits keep well away!

The young usually don't travel far from where they fledged. They are keen to take advantage of the food we leave out and the nestboxes we put up, which are useful if natural tree-holes are in short supply.

LONG-TAILED TIT ▲

This beautiful little bird looks like a tiny ball of feathers with a long tail sticking out of the rear. Covered with moss and lichen and stitched together with cobwebs, the long-tailed tits' nest also has to be one of the most beautiful structures in the natural world.

The nests are designed to be perfectly camouflaged in the forks of trees or hedgerows. Here the parents, often with the help of aunts, uncles and siblings from previous years, will help raise a brood of six to eight chicks. With long-tailed tits, raising a brood is most definitely a family affair!

CITY BIRDS

SONG THRUSH ▶

The shrubberies and lawns in town parks and gardens offer the perfect bed and breakfast for the spotty song thrush. An expert at digging up earthworms and smashing open snail shells to get to the meat inside, the song thrush is also more than happy to eat fruits and berries from trees when other food becomes scarce in the winter.

◀ GREENFINCH

The greenfinch is a keen seed-eater, and has been tempted into towns and gardens by all the free food we put out for birds. With a chunky body and a large bill designed to crack tough seeds, greenfinches often use their size to push off smaller birds from feeders, as they fly down and dominate the best perches.

CHAFFINCH ▶

One of the most common and widespread British birds, the chaffinch can be found wherever trees or bushes are present. The male, with his blue-grey head and pinkish breast, can easily be told apart from the much duller female. Unlike the greenfinch, the chaffinch is often happiest feeding on the ground, as it hoovers up all the food spilt from the feeders by other birds.

DUNNOCK ▲

You will often find a dunnock creeping around on the ground like a mouse, nervously flicking its wings. Many people mistake it for a sparrow. It likes a mix of woodland, scrub and farmland, so gardens are the perfect habitat for this streaky brown and grey bird. While some broods are reared by a single male and female, other nests seem to be part of a very modern family, with a number of fathers and mothers!

CITY BIRDS

Lots of other birds – originally just visitors to Britain – find towns and cities are able to offer a very comfortable lifestyle too.

RING-NECKED PARAKEETS ▶

These birds are the most exotic and colourful visitors to our garden bird tables. Originally from the mountains of India, these beautiful and noisy birds can mostly be seen in suburban London and surrounding towns.

Ring-necked parakeets prefer to nest in tree holes, and their aggressive nature means birds like little owls and jackdaws can often be ejected where space is limited. Their messy fruit and seed-eating habits have also made them very unpopular at some garden bird feeders.

Parakeets will often dominate feeders

COLLARED DOVE

Collared doves are so common in our towns, churchyards and parks that it is astonishing to think the first time they bred here was only about 60 years ago. Having found their own way to Britain from the continent, they have since spread to most places where they can find seeds and berries.

Collared doves usually raise a clutch of two chicks. They aren't very good at building nests, so many nests fail. They may try to breed up to five times a year, making them firm believers in the phrase 'if at first you don't succeed, then try and try again'!

▼

A collared dove's call is a three-part cooing sound

CITY BUTTERFLIES

Many of Britain's butterflies are strong flyers, and are surprisingly abundant in lots of towns and cities. They are attracted by garden flowers and floral displays in public parks.

PEACOCK ▶

No other British butterfly has the startling eye-spots of the peacock butterfly. A common sight in urban gardens during the spring and summer, these long-lived butterflies hibernate in sheds before emerging to mate in the following spring. The female will then lay her green eggs on nettles.

LARGE WHITE ▶

The large white butterfly is the bigger of the two butterflies known as the 'cabbage whites'. These butterflies are very unpopular with vegetable growers, because of their habit of leaving cabbage leaves full of holes. It is actually the hungry caterpillars that do all the damage, before finally wandering off to spend the winter as a chrysalis.

RED ADMIRAL ▶

One of Britain's largest and most magnificent butterflies, the red admiral does not live here all year round but migrates here in the summer from the continent. In good years they can arrive in huge numbers. As they are strong fliers, they are attracted to anywhere with large numbers of nectar-rich flowers, such as in parks and gardens.

COMMA ▲

Once a very rare butterfly along the Welsh-English border, the comma has now spread over England and Wales, and is currently marching up through Scotland at a rapid pace. The ragged outline to its wing makes the comma immediately obvious when it is at rest. Its name comes from the distinctive silver mark on the underside of the hindwing, which makes the butterfly look like a dried leaf. This is the perfect camouflage when hiding from predators in the winter.

BEES, WASPS, SLUGS AND SNAILS

These insects have all learnt that living on our doorsteps can be a very profitable business.

HONEY BEE ▶

The honey bee is a familiar insect in both the town and country. In order to make honey, humans have been keeping bees in man-made beehives for thousands of years. Each beehive holds a queen and several tens of thousands of workers, whose job it is to collect pollen and nectar between early spring and autumn. This food will help feed both the workers back at the hive and the developing larvae. With plenty of flowers to be found in our towns and cities, urban hives certainly make tasty honey too!

COMMON WASP ▼

Well known for building their huge papery nests in our lofts in the spring and bothering us in the summer, many people consider wasps little more than a pain – or a sting! But in order to feed their larvae, wasps carry out a valuable service of controlling many of the pests in our parks and gardens.

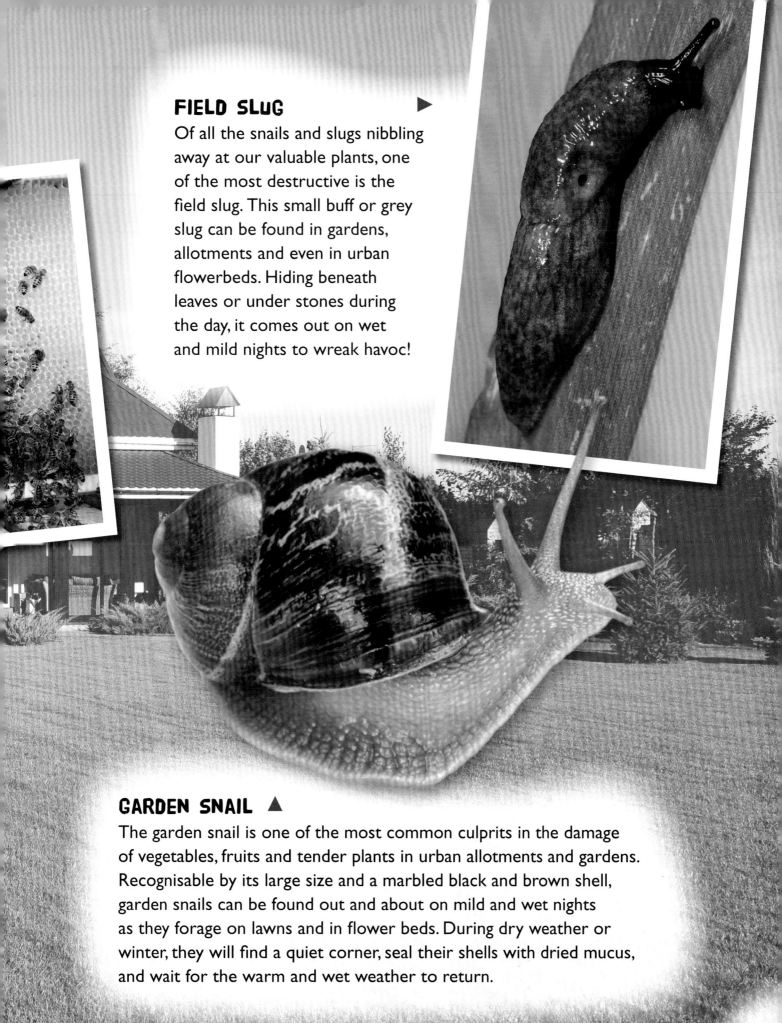

FIELD SLUG ▶

Of all the snails and slugs nibbling away at our valuable plants, one of the most destructive is the field slug. This small buff or grey slug can be found in gardens, allotments and even in urban flowerbeds. Hiding beneath leaves or under stones during the day, it comes out on wet and mild nights to wreak havoc!

GARDEN SNAIL ▲

The garden snail is one of the most common culprits in the damage of vegetables, fruits and tender plants in urban allotments and gardens. Recognisable by its large size and a marbled black and brown shell, garden snails can be found out and about on mild and wet nights as they forage on lawns and in flower beds. During dry weather or winter, they will find a quiet corner, seal their shells with dried mucus, and wait for the warm and wet weather to return.

Feeding frenzy
No matter how urban a
location, a few feeders will
always pull in the birds!

URBAN NATURE WORDS

abundant – common (great numbers of)

agility – moving quickly and easily

aquatic – living in or near water

basking – lying in the warmth

climate – normal pattern of weather through the year in a certain place

colonies – groups

colonise – spread throughout an area

copses – small groups of trees

DDT – a chemical that was used for killing insects

extinct – died out

feral – animals brought from another place in captivity, which have become
   wild after being released or escaping

foraging – searching for food

hibernation – a long deep sleep during winter

hover – float in the air without moving

impenetrable – impossible to get through

insectivorous – feeding on insects

lowland – an area of land that is lower than the surrounding land

mange – a skin disease

membrane – a thin layer of tissue

nectar – a sugary fluid found in many flowers

on the wing – in the air

pesticides – chemicals used to kill insects that are harmful to plants

plumage – feathers

predators – animals that prey on other animals

rubble – bits of loose rock or bricks, usually from buildings

scavengers – animals that feed on rubbish, dead plants or dead animals

sewers – underground channels that carry away drainage water and waste

shoals – large numbers of fish swimming together

territorial – defending territory strongly

urban – of a city or town

verges – edges

warren – burrow where rabbits live

wingspan – the measurement across a bird's wings from tip to tip

INDEX

BRANCH	DATE
WH	12/12